RAILROAD CAMP

Adolf Hungry Wolf

In Tribute to a now-gone place of drama and character in the Northwest woods

(Front cover) A memorable day at a historic location: Railroad Camp in August 1961, seen from the slippery platform of the big trackside water tank. It was then among the last places a boy could go during high school summer vacation to witness a real steam railroad show of this caliber.
AHW photo

(Opposite) Here is the best-known photo showing Railroad Camp, taken in 1942, with virtually the complete Polson Brothers locomotive roster lined up. Former Northern Pacific Mallet No. 3100 is on the mainline with a load of logs. Other engines, from left to right, include Shay No. 3 (in foreground); much bigger Shay No. 91 to right; a couple of the smaller rod engines; Shay No. 33; Prairie No. 45 (in foreground); Mikado 101; a Consolidation; a pair of Mikados (Nos. 90 and 70 to the right of No. 3100); Shay No. 191 (behind them); plus another engine way back inside the shop. In addition, the first bladed Caterpillar bought by Polson is sitting on a flatcar behind No. 90. Second track from the left was known as the caboose track. Cabooses were stored on the far end over the weekends, then pulled up to the freight house on Monday mornings and loaded with meat and supplies for logging camps along the way.
C. Kinsey photo

(Right) Another special moment from that summer vacation visit to Railroad Camp in 1961, as Mallet No. 120 approaches the water tank after one of several rain showers. Borrowing the title from David P. Morgan's book "Steam's Finest Hour," a mounted print of this shot won a high school prize, then afterwards decorated my father's study, evidence perhaps that he had properly passed on from himself and his father our shared first names and a passion for picture taking.
AHW photo

Printed in Canada by Kromar Printing Ltd.
Typesetting by Communications Plus

ISBN 0-920698-43-3

For additional copies of this book, or a list of our Canadian books, calendars, cards, tapes and videos, write to:
Canadian Caboose Press
Box 844, Skookumchuck, B.C.
V0B 2E0 - Canada

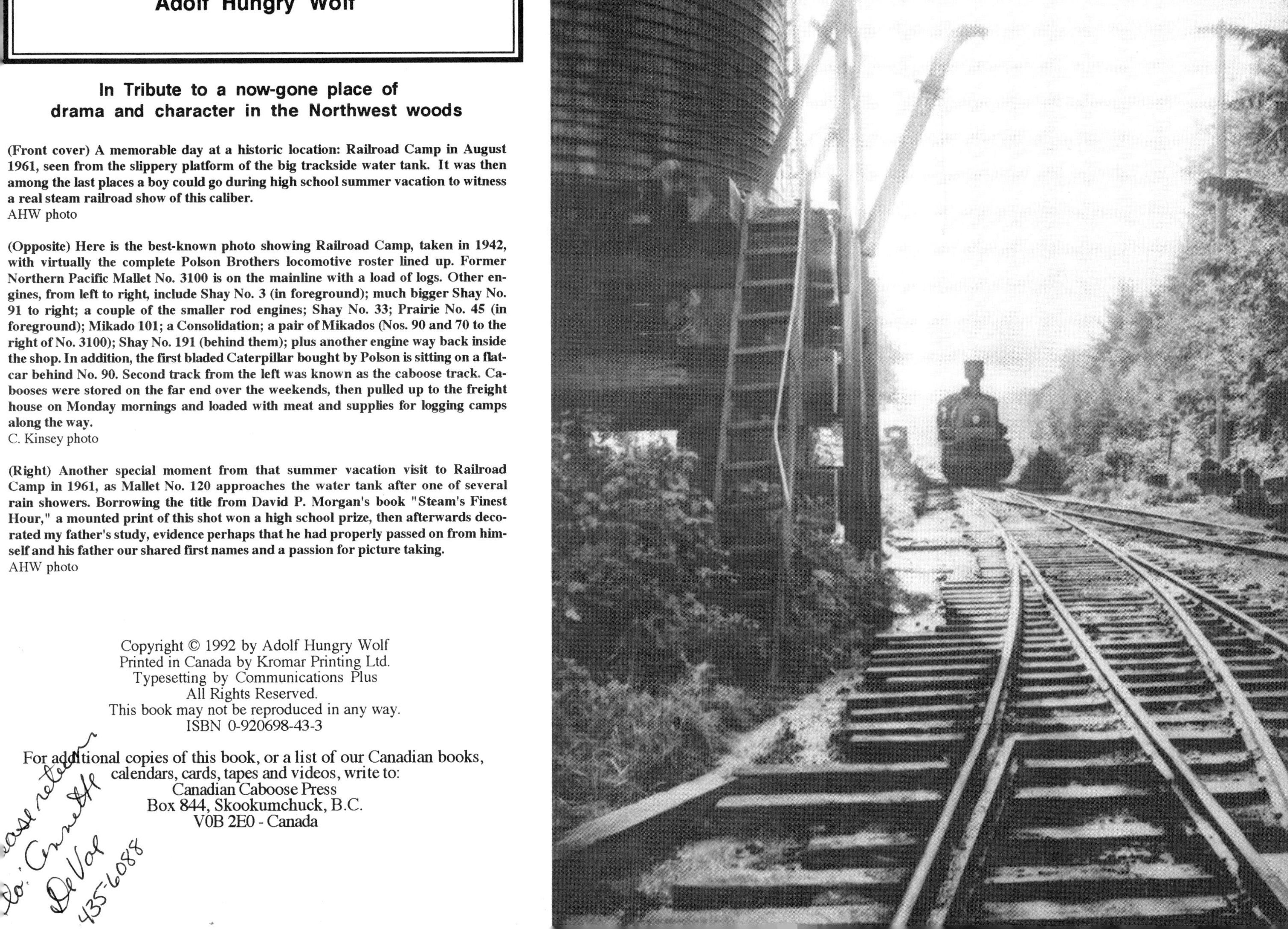

(Above, both pages) Nine engines were posed at Railroad Camp for this panoramic view taken in the 1920's. Centre of attention is the train of logs parked on the mainline, in charge of Baldwin Ten-wheeler No. 18, a rather unusual engine for such duty. Built in 1901 for the Arizona & New Mexico RR and bought by Polson in 1918, she was later relegated to work train service. Her final years were spent rusting in the weeds on the rip tracks near the left of this picture. Loggers, engine crews and kitchen staff are all around her, with "Ol' Betsy" parked on the next track over.
William D. Jones , Historical Coll'n

POLSON BROTHERS LOGGING COMPANY

Building a railroad in the middle of nowhere

Two Canadian brothers from Nova Scotia named Alex and Robert Polson went to the Pacific Northwest in the late 1800s to look for land and timber opportunities. They first formed the Hoquiam Timber Company, purchasing vast stands of immense trees in an area north of Grays Harbor, which were then cut down and processed through their Polson Brothers Logging Company. The Railroad Camp of this book became headquarters for their operation, a unique place deep in the woods where workers and their families lived right by their jobs, a village where boys played on trains they grew up to run.

Initially, logging was done by men using axes and handsaws, then pulling the immense logs through the forests with teams of oxen. The machine age soon brought steam-powered "donkeys" and skidders, followed by locomotives that hauled the trees aboard long, winding trains. By 1903 there were seven miles of standard gauge tracks from the Polson's riverfront log dumping site at New London (a few miles by water from their mill at Hoquiam) to a clearing in the forest known as Railroad Camp.

The first engine bought by the Polson's still exists today, a little 0-4-0 saddletanker built in 1880 by Porter. Polson crews called it "Ol' Betsy," but history knows it better as the Northern Pacific Railroad's "Minnetonka," first locomotive to come west over Washington's Cascade Mountains. After 30 years of logging service, the engine went back to the Northern Pacific in 1933 (for cash and a bigger engine). It's now in Chicago, kept by Burlington Northern for historical purposes.

From such an auspicious beginning, the Polson roster soon grew to include a variety of rod-driven and geared locomotives, some bought new, many others obtained second-hand. Shays and Climaxes worked the rougher branchlines, while mainline trains were first handled by a pair of old Ten-Wheelers, then by Consolidations, Mikados and eventually by big Mallets. Wooden skeleton trucks were followed by others made of steel, then by a variety of solid log cars that numbered several hundred.

As the Polson railroad expanded, loggers moved further away from Railroad Camp into the woods, followed by strings of bunk cars that provided nearby housing, along with room for cooking and dining, light shopwork, even offices. These were built at Railroad Camp, which continued to be the operation's focal point. Some of these portable camps moved out along branchlines, while others were parked on sidings along the mainline itself. One important branch ran to the coastal town of Moclips, where it met the Northern Pacific Railroad for an outside connection.

The mainline through Polson property was completed just before World War II when it reached Crane Creek, near scenic Lake Quinault, some 45 rail miles from the log dump at New London and about 38 miles from Railroad Camp. At that time, Polson bought one of the biggest engines ever used by a logging railroad, former Northern Pacific No. 3100, a 1910 Baldwin 2-6-2 Mallet compound, for which they paid $10,000. At 305,150 lbs. this became the heaviest engine ever to run on the line, its tractive effort of 58,100 lbs. making

t also among the strongest. After the war broke out and railroad traffic became extra heavy, Northern Pacific is said to have offered more than eight times its selling price to get this big engine back, but the Polson's preferred to keep it running on their line.

In 1948 the Polson operation was sold to Rayonier Incorporated, which had been formed in 1937 and was already operating another logging railroad further north in the state, after buying out the Olympic peninsula holdings of the Bloedel-Donovan Lumber Mills. Rubber-tired trucks were becoming more efficient at reaching logging sites than geared engines running over rough branchlines, but the Rayonier company felt that its mainline railroads were still best for the long hauls. Thus, Railroad Camp remained the headquarters of a busy logging railroad until steam engines were finally replaced by diesels, which happened in the late 1960s. At that time a new mainline was built to bypass the old buildings, which were then torn down. After some ten more years of running only with diesels, Rayonier closed the mainline itself in 1985, then pulled up the tracks, selling some of the equipment and scrapping the rest. As a result, the photos on these pages document a way of life in the woods that will never be seen again.

(Below) Only 40 years passed between the two pictures on these pages, yet life had changed so tremendously. Steam was still on hand in the summer of 1964, when I went back for a second time to the spot from where I took the front cover photo. Fresh-painted yellow and green Baldwin diesel No. 90 stands front and centre, indicating who is now in charge of Rayonier's mainline; some steam was still used for switching and work trains.
AHW photo

(Above) Woodburning days at Railroad Camp, circa 1910. Here are crews and shopmen with eight of their engines fired up and ready to go. From left to right: 2-6-2 No. 45 and an early caboose; famous 0-4-OT "Old Betsy; "4-6-0 No. 10; 2-8-0 No. 99; Shay No. 55; Climax Nos. 11 and 12; plus Shay No. 33.
H.G. Nelson photo/Rayonier collection

(Left) Dressed in their Sunday finest, these two couples of the 1920s illustrate how trains and daily life were mixed into one for the folks at Railroad Camp.
Bobby Rogers collection
(Opposite) Home life at Railroad Camp included flowers and vegetable gardens, along with train rides to visit neighbors at logging camps up and down the line.
Bobby Rogers collection

GROWING UP IN RAILROAD CAMP

Told by Bobby Rogers
(aboard No. 76, while running from the landing at New London
to Crane Creek in 1980, hauling 39 empties, a caboose and a water car).

"Railroad Camp was my childhood home; our family lived in one of the company houses d that's where I grew up. There were about 40 families living there at the time; our house is right by a big redwood and the schoolhouse was nearby, although it was done away with the mid-thirties and after that we kids were sent to school in Hoquiam by bus. There have en Rogers' on this RR for 71 years.

"We did a lot of playing on and around the railroad equipment. I suppose you could say it is dangerous, but I don't remember any of us ever getting hurt. The company tried to dis-urage it, but they never really stopped us. We were used to being around trains right from start, so we knew pretty well how to be careful. Everybody at Railroad Camp rode on the ins; there were no motor roads in the earlier days, so trains were the main ways we had for tting around.

"Both of my grandfathers worked at Railroad Camp long before I was born. My mother is about 14 or 15 when she moved there with her parents; that's where she met my dad and ere they made their home together. We'd have church services every Sunday at the school-use; a lady came out from town to conduct them. Two delivery trucks came out every day th groceries and supplies, since the nearest store was at Axford Prairie. The Polson family pt what we called the "white house" at Railroad Camp (most of the houses were red) for itors and guests, where they got free room and board. In addition to the families, there re a lot of single men living at Railroad Camp. Polson maintained about 40 family houses re, plus about 50 bunk cars with six to eight men in each, most of them working on the ilroad. The loggers usually lived out at the different camps. On the railroad, the section n were mostly Greeks, while the enginemen were Swedes. There were 12 to 15 camps out the woods in those days - about one camp every five miles or so. The loggers and railroad-s were all friends - it was a neighborly relationship at Railroad Camp and all along the Pol-n line. Often my mother would take the morning train from Railroad Camp up to Humptu-s or one of the other camps and spend the day visiting in the cookhouse with the ladies, changing gossip and so forth, then she'd come back home on another train at the end of day.

"My mother had a close call riding trains one time. She was aboard a train of logs head-g from Railroad Camp to Log City. In those days they would put the caboose up next to engine; the brakemen had to climb back over the loaded cars to get at the brakes. On s trip, the brakeman decided to ride on top of the logs of the last car, to save having to mb back there. He was a good friend of the family, so he asked my mom to ride back there th him, but she didn't. When the train got down to its destination the third car from the ar split the switch, causing the loads to pile up, which killed that brakeman.

"Another time she fell off the train and was lucky to be unhurt. She'd left Railroad Camp oard the caboose of this train, and when they got going the engineer waved for her to me up to the cab - I think it was No. 45. She jumped from the caboose platform to the en-ne pilot, but her pleated skirt got caught on the brake stem of the caboose. She fell clear wn into a culvert, but by the time they stopped the train she was up and walking.

"I always figured to work on the railroad - my dad wanted me and my brother both to fol-w in his footsteps, but my brother didn't want to get his hands dirty, so he went into the urance business instead. My first day as a fireman was aboard the old No. 45 on a work in. Of course, having grown up around the engines I knew all about it - I rode engines all time, live on them. We were laying steel between Railroad Camp and Camp 14, so I yed around that engine all week. Although she was an oilburner by that time, the darned

old thing would only keep steam up for three or four hours, so I'd have to set my alarm and get up in the middle of the night to look after it. In other words, I'd have to fire it all day long, then stay up half the night to babybsit it besides. And in those days we often had 14 and 16 hour days - 12 hours nearly all the time. Our pay was $1.50 an hour. We'd get off Sat-urdays, but as a young man I usually had to work as hostler on Sundays, getting the engines steamed up for the next day.

"Men were regularly killed back when it was standard to have cabooses up next to the en-gines; the brakemen had to climb over the loaded cars to set brakes on each hill - usually six or eight times per trip; the cars in those days had no air brakes. The men wore cork shoes to get over the logs, but then they slipped on the steel cars. Mostly we had disconnects back then. Polson was nearly shut down several times, due to dangers and accidents. They didn't hire married men as brakemen on account of that. Another danger was tightening the brake wheels on the cars - if the chain broke, that was it; they usually lost their balance and went over.

The last brakeman that I know of died in 1949 at Log City. They were putting together two loads of 20 cars each to make one train. This fellow - he was about 30 or so - walked be-tween the knuckles and got coupled into the train. The head brakeman went back to see where this guy had gone and found him still alive. But the pins had already dropped on the couplers, so when he pulled it up and got the cars uncoupled, the poor guy just dropped dead. My dad had to come over with the No. 70 to get his body.

No. 70 was my dad's regular engine for many years, until he retired in 1957. Very few others ever got to run it during his time; he took care of it as if it were his own. For instance, instead of painting the boiler jacket black like the other engines, he kept it blued just like a rifle barrel; he got his own tallow just to shine that boiler jacket up. Also, it was the only engine that didn't have its rods painted - he greased them and kept the metal shiny. Every Friday night after work he'd oil the whole engine so it wouldn't rust over the weekend. I think he took better care of that engine than he did my mother. She always knew when dad was coming with his engine, - even back when we had 10, 12 trains through Railroad Camp every day. Mom would always know dad's whistle; he had a distinct way of making it sound.

No 132
Polsons Hoglers.
C. Kinsey Photo – Seattle

"My grandpa worked in the shops at Railroad Camp when I was a kid; I grew up seeing im working on all those engines and then later I ran some of them. I never ran the Minnetonka" - she was gone before my time - but my grandpa overhauled that engine efore it was taken to the Chicago World's Fair in 1939, then he went back there with my randma to see her. The company had traded this old engine back to the Northern Pacific r No. 51, a big Consolidation that came here as a coal burner. The coal didn't work out, a couple years later they changed her to burn oil, then the boiler split, so they just ent her off to scrap. She wasn't here for long.

"First engine I ever ran was No. 99, another Consolidation. She had no trailing heels, so she used to jump the track a lot. They finally parked her for a year or so, then ey did some work on her running gear and after that she was o.k. But I found it a hard ngine to run - I was little and it had a stiff Johnson Bar that I could hardly pull back.

"When No. 90 arrived, old Robert Polson was so proud that he just stood out on the orch of his office at Railroad Camp, fingers hooked in is suspenders, with Ninety parked right out front. He laimed, 'This engine will haul every log on the penin- ula.' It weighed 86-tons and was the heaviest on the ne. It could haul about 30 loads, while the other Mika- os, Nos. 2, 70 and 101 could haul about 20, same as o. 99.

"They sent my dad down to Longview to look over e Weyerhaeuser engines when No. 120 was bought. e said they had a couple that were way bigger, but they ouldn't have made it through our bridges. In those ays engines came up here on the Northern Pacific to Moclips.

"In a lot of ways this was a family operation. For in- tance, my mom was the banker for all the train crews. hey'd give her their pay to put in the bank; she'd bring ack whatever cash they wanted, in gold coins.

"On time the lumber market was so bad that Polson couldn't pay dad for six months - st groceries - then later he gave him all the back pay. But men who got fired had to alk from Railroad Camp down to the Landing and then get across. In the Twenties two en were fired on a Friday and that weekend a small bridge was burned down. On Monday orning No. 45 went over into the hole it left and killed the fireman.

"There was a bad wreck at Camp 6 around 1940 that killed four men. No. 99 was going ome light to Railroad Camp on a Friday night. The brakeman tried to reach the dis- atcher on the phone but couldn't, so he gave a highball and they just took off. In those ays they used plug-in telephones to check in at each stop with the dispatcher. On the ay, No. 90 suddenly met a speeder and they hit head-on. My dad was uphill from there n No. 70, waiting to get clearance, and he saw it all coming but couldn't do anything bout it.

"It's surprising there weren't more accidents; there sure were plenty of dangers. For in- tance, the No. 3100 would leave Railroad Camp at three in the morning with 70 empties nd my dad would leave 15 minutes later with the No. 70 and another 30 empties. It'd be ark and storming and they couldn't see a thing - those black log cars didn't show up at ll, with no caboose on the back, or marker lamps.

"A brakeman was killed at Camp 14 one night in a storm. He was riding the point ith his lantern, shoving empties around a curve. He was standing up and suddenly hit is head on a tree that was blown part way down over the tracks. The engine kept shov- g, until the fireman noticed the lit lantern laying by the tracks and got the engineer to stop, but it was too late.

"On the branch north of Moclips there used to be a tie mill that cut all the ties for the railroad; it was owned by the company. Just before that mill the tracks went east and crossed Highway 101 and we were always hitting vehicles there. My dad killed two or three at that place. We had a water tank there, and once I was stopped with the engine and 50 loads, which hung out over the highway. It was night and a truck driver didn't see the cars, so he drove right through the train. It was a miracle that he survived.

"My dad turned his No. 70 over one time, shoving empties uphill at one of the land- ings. A rail broke and let the engine down; my dad broke his leg, but nothing worse. Funny thing is, a couple of years ago I did the same thing with a pair of the diesels. Num- bers 76 and 90 turned part way over when I had them on a long train, and I broke my an- kle.

"One time around 1950 a crew tried to drop a loaded tank car (to uncouple it on the run) above Camp 14, but it had no handbrake so it got away. I was stopped for water down by the Quinault River, with the crummy towards Crane Creek. We had a train of logs and the brakeman was about three cars from the end, setting up the retainers, when that tank car came rolling up quietly and smacked the caboose, setting it on fire.

"Around 1960 they wanted to see what No. 120 could pull, so they gave me 90 empties. When we got to Camp 14 the engine was slipping so bad that the dispatcher said he could see the rail shifting back and forth underneath. We had to drop off part of the train. Going through Camp 14 I could make the No. 90 slip and then bark so loud that it would knock windows out on the bunk cars!

"Another time the Superintendent wanted to see if No. 2 and 101 could pull 100 empties north, together. They were doing al- right until they got to the Quinault River - a mountain had slid down across the tracks during the night. They were pushing so hard that No. 101 went right through the piled up dirt, but got derailed. They were lucky no one was killed.

"One time No. 70 had the valve stem on the whistle overhauled over the weekend. When I took it out on Monday and blew the whistle, it got stuck open; the stem was too big. So I had to put waste in my ears and go up to hit it with a hammer, to get it unstuck. From that I became nerve deaf in one ear; it was sure something shrill.

"They used to station some of the engines out along the line. Two or three stayed at Camp 14 - often No. 70 and one or two Shays to work the spurs. Another was kept at Camp 3, also at Camp 6. These would stay for the week, then come into Railroad Camp on weekends for repairs and service. No. 3100 was mainly used between Camp 14 and Railroad Camp. Lighter engines brought the cars to the Landing the next day.

"Alco brought a 660 hp demonstrator to Railroad Camp in the early 1950s. They had my dad run it, but of course he didn't know anything about diesels. They had him pull 45 empties to Camp 14, but he couldn't get the sanders to work so they kept stalling. They tried it on the Camp 3 line too, where there were still Shays working. We finally got die- sels in 1962, and that was the beginning of the end for Railroad Camp. Mom and I lived there until 1969, when all the steam was gone and the company closed up the place. We were offered a house up at Crane Creek, but my mom decided we'd move into Hoquiam in- stead.

(Above) Some of the fathers and grandfathers of boys who grew up to work at Railroad Camp, posed on No. 99 in about 1930.
Bobby Rogers collection.

101
99
Polson Logging

A RAILROAD CAMP GALLERY

From the 1920s

(Opposite) Two Polson crews and a pair of Baldwin engines are posed at the end of Railroad Camp's servicing tracks, just a few feet from dense forests. Mikado No. 101 and Consolidation No. 99 came new to the line in 1912 and 1905, working side by side until their retirement in the 1950s and eventual scrapping on the spot.

(Above) Loggers were known to have great appetites and logging railroaders were probably not far behind, so that logging camp kitchens like this one were kept busy almost around the clock. An unusual feature in this kitchen is the brakewheel on the far wall, proof that there is a pair of trucks under the floor, as well. Most Polson buildings were portable units kept parked on tracks, with home base being Railroad Camp.

(Right) The tables are set with places for about 60 men and a variety of homemade foods including pies and cakes for dessert. These views are part of a series taken on the Polson property around 1920.

Both pages, H.G. Nelson photos/Rayonier collection

(Both pages) Some of the men and equipment responsible for keeping the steam-powered Polson Logging Company in operation, as seen inside Railroad Camp's main machine shop. These crews could build most anything needed on the tracks and in the woods, demonstrating a form of self-sufficiency that can only be envied by companies nowadays. Note that all machinery is driven by belts and pulleys, which are connected to a steam-powered plant outside the building. The unprotected gears and open-faced grinders would give nightmares to modern safety inspectors.
H.G. Nelson photos/Rayonier collection

Machine Shop
R R Camp
Logging Co
-6-

(Both pages) More portraits of the skilled craftsmen who kept the Polson Logging show on the move. Here's the blacksmith shop and adjacent car shop at Railroad Camp, where the growing and changing rolling stock of the company was maintained and repaired. Starting in 1903 with a dozen disconnect log trucks like those on the facing page, the Polson line eventually saw hundreds of cars, many of which were built with new or second-hand parts here in these shops. Disconnect trucks were handy when long logs were needed for the market, since they could be adjusted in pairs underneath. However, this same independence also helped them to come off the tracks quite regularly, especially when they were placed under trees so long that their mid-sections dragged on the ties.
H.G. Nelson photos/Rayonier collection

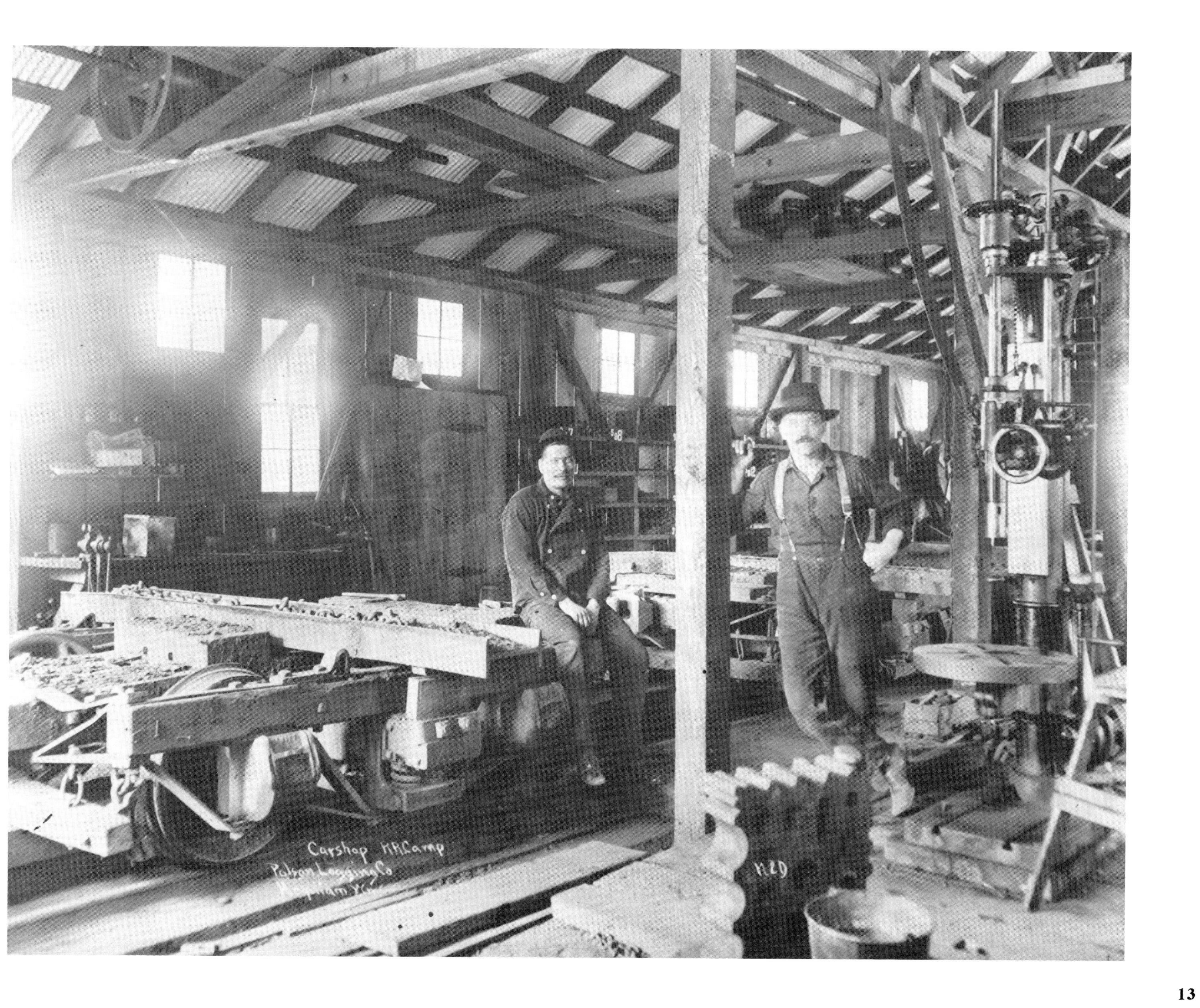
Carshop RR Camp
Polson Logging Co

olson Logging Company

SCENES ALONG THE LINE

ght) When tracks were new from Railroad mp to Camp 3 and Camp 7. At a quick glance it pears that this forest has some pretty good-sized es, but look at the stump on the left to see what d to grow here. A rail bicycle just like this one nained parked outside the dispatcher's office at ilroad Camp right up to the final seasons, after ich it was sent to the British Columbia Forest seum as a unique artifact.

pposite, above) The first engine bought by the lson Brothers for their new logging railroad was s simple 0-4-0 saddletanker, which became own as "Ol' Betsy." That was certainly a loss in tus, since the 1880 Porter originally worked the rthern Pacific Railroad's mainline under the me "Minnetonka," earning fame as the first lo- notive to cross the Cascade Mountains. This an- ue is now kept in Chicago by the Burlington rthern for historical purposes.

pposite, below) Also bought second-hand from Northern Pacific at the beginning of the Polson ging railroad's operations was No. 10, a mainline n-wheeler seen here taking on a load of wood at neside fuel stop. It's sad to think how many an- nt trees this engine alone burned up before being verted to run on oil. Those blocks were sawn by nd, then split with light, double-bladed axes. If 1've cut firewood with a chainsaw and splitting ul, you can appreciate the work it took to keep a t of woodburners rolling over the tracks.
3. Nelson/Rayonier collection

(Left) "Western Terminus - Polson Brothers Railroad," says the pencilled note with this print. It shows Ten-wheeler No. 10 with crewmen and a couple of ladies on a trestle still under construction.

(Opposite) Another shot of No. 10 during railroad construction on the Polson logging line. Four-wheeled dump cars are being loaded with earth at one place to be used as fill in another. Polson's two 4-6-0's spent much of their careers with work trains, after heavier power replaced them from log hauling duties.

H.G. Nelson photos/Rayonier collection

Polson Logging Co.
Hoquiam Wn. 4

(Opposite) Filling a log car was quite a project back when there was a lot of manpower needed to help the steam machine and its cable lines of rigging to heft around mighty trees, even if they had already been cut up into five or six pieces. There was a lot of camaraderie among logging outfits like Polson's in part due to the brotherhood of looking out for each other's lives in an age of dangerous work and little compensation.

(Above) This was the Polson's first big step forward in the way of mainline locomotive power, after working with second-hand Ten-wheelers and the old tanker Minnetonka. Consolidation No. 99 was bought new from Baldwin in 1905 and was for some time queen of the engines on the line, weighing in at 137,000 pounds and giving out with 29.200 lbs. of tractive effort. The engine was scrapped at Railroad Camp in 1959. Note the interesting pieced-together stack.
H. G. Nelson photos/Rayonier collection

10
POLSON BROS. LOGGING CO.

Polson's Ten-Wheelers

(Opposite) In the early days of the logging railroad, Polson's No. 10 was one of the regular mainline engines, here hauling some mighty logs on disconnect trucks. This type of engine was not common on logging railroads, but the Polson operation kept two in service through most of its years. Note that the company name is on both the tender and cab sides.
Rayonier collection

(Above) Here's No. 10 in the final seasons of life, sitting forlorn and partly dismantled on the rip track at Railroad Camp in June 1952.
Railway Negative Exchange/AHW collection

(Right) Taken at the same time and place, but a little further down the track, this shot shows 4-6-0 No. 18, sporting a tender much different from that with which she left the Baldwin Locomotive Works for an initial stint on the Arizona New Mexico Railroad. Still relatively intact, the engine had apparently not been out of service too long in 1952.
Railway Negative Exchange/AHW collection

(Above) Handsome two-truck Shay No. 33 was built for Polson in 1905 and scrapped at Railroad Camp in 1947. Originally a wood-burner with a big stack, she is seen here with a new oil bunker on her tender and a plain straight stack.

(Opposite) Out in the woods on the Polson Brother's logging line, we see the dangerous work of loading heavy logs on skeleton-framed log cars, which by this time in the 1920s had pretty well replaced the earlier disconnects. One steam-powered skidder is being used to lift the logs, while another sits idle nearby. One of the two Climax engines is switching the cars in the background. Notice the freshly-laid tracks, back when these were still being built as operations progressed through the woods, taken up again when the trees were gone and put down somewhere else. Geared engines like this Climax were used on these rougher, more temporary branches. If those big tongs rip out of that log, at least two fellows will be in for a sudden jolt.
Both, H.G. Nelson photos/Rayonier collection

(Above) Southern end of the Polson logging line was here at New London, better known to crews as "Log City," just a few miles from the company mill at Hoquiam. A steam-powered unloading machine was kept busy dumping logs from trains of railroad cars into the river so they could be floated downstream for processing.

(Opposite) Another site where Polson logs were dumped directly into water was at Moclips on the Pacific Coast, reached by a branch from Railroad Camp that also connected with Northern Pacific Railroad tracks. The primitive unloading machine was built by Polson shopmen at Railroad Camp.
Both, H.G. Nelson photos/Rayonier collection

Unloading Cars On Landing
Polson Logging Co
Hoquiam Wash

A Shay and Two Climaxes

(Left) For many years the smallest engine on the Polson roster was two-truck Sh No. 3, built in 1910 as Kootenay Logging No. 2 and first operated in Canada, not f from where this book is being made. Occasionally used for switching and work tra service until its retirement in the late 1950s, this fine machine is on display at Pro ised Land Park, along the highway north of Hoquiam, not far from the former Ra road Camp.
Jones photo; Aberdeen, Washington

(Above) A pair of almost identical two-truck Climax geared engines were bought the Polson Brothers to operate over rougher sections of their logging line, which w a Climax specialty. Here's No. 12 out in the woods around 1920.
Mike Kessler Collection

(Opposite) Climax No. 11 looks quite new in this picture, although the print gives date or other details. Disconnect trucks are still being used under the logs; the f car ahead of the engine appears to be a mainline model, probably brought in fro the Northern Pacific interchange at Moclips.
H.G. Nelson photo/Rayonier collection

11

RAYONIER
20

The Rayonier Era at Railroad Camp

(Opposite) Saddletank 2-6-6-2 No. 110 is over the drop-pit inside the main locomotive shop at Railroad Camp in 1956, a stack of nearby tires attesting to serious wheel work in progress. Mallet No. 120 stands in the doorway, bedded down for the night. Eight years earlier, Rayonier Incorporated took over the Polson Logging Company, including Railroad Camp.
an Kistler photo

(Right) Truly a "framed portrait," showing one of Rayonier's boilermakers taking a moment's break for the photographer. His work consisted of replacing bricks inside the firebox of Rayonier Mallet No. 14 at Railroad Camp.
nie Plant collection

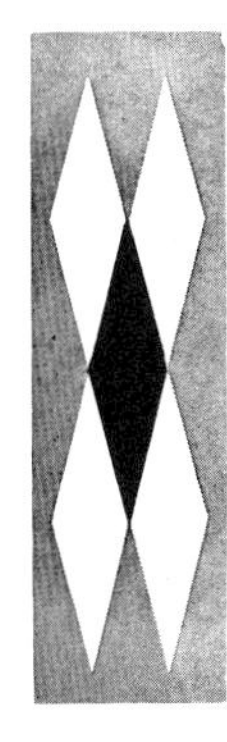

70

RAYONIER

RAYONIER
INCORPORATED

Opposite, upper left) Railroad Camp was a rail photographer's paradise in the years after most other places were dieselized, as there were always steam locomotives fired up to keep the logs rolling. Here's Mikado No. 70 going for water, with a close-up of the engineer on duty in the cab.

Opposite below) Mallet No. 14 pushes one of the distinctive cabooses past the Railroad Camp water tank towards the yard, where one of the other Mallets is barely seen switching.

Opposite, right) Here's the famous view again, this time with Mikado No. 90 on the mainline towing a work train for track repair, including a flat car with rails and frogs, plus three old dump cars for ballast.

our photos, Ernie Plant collection

Above) Probably the single most photographed spot at Railroad Camp and along the whole line was right here, outside the main locomotive shop, where active engines were usually parked between assignments. On this day, Mallet Nos. 14 and 120 face each other in the company of much smaller Mikado No. 2.

Ernie Plant collection

Right) Somewhat like a centipede, No. 38 weaves its long body through the trackage at Railroad Camp, headed down into the yard with a couple of hitchhikers, log scalers going to check out the next train load. This practice of riding engine footboards was probably frowned upon by company officials even then; now it is against safety regulations in most places. The engine had just arrived at Railroad Camp not long before this June 1956 photo, after a gloried tour of duty with California's famous Sierra Railroad.

Stan Kistler photo

Three Old Timers at Railroad Camp

(Left) Built in 1906, Prairie-type 2-6-2 No. 45 was exactly 50 years old at th time of this scene, switching cars on a rainy day. In a few more seasons the en gine was retired and put on display in the nearby city of Hoquiam.

(Above) "Camp mother" and cook "par excellence" for many years at Rai road Camp was Julia Johnson, seen here preparing an evening meal for 60 hu gry loggers. Her cookhouse was parked on tracks sitting on railroad wheel while her home was in one of the company houses nearby.

(Opposite) Dispatcher Paul Pauly checks on the phone at his desk if there is an more work that needs to be done, while the engineer of Mallet No. 38 awai permission to tie up for the day. Note the map near the dispatcher's left elbov with thumb tacks marking places where trains and work crews were locate By this time all engines were equipped with two-way radios, allowing immediat contact with trains out on the line. Paul Pauly worked logging trains starting i 1919 until he fell from one and broke his back, after which he became Railroa Camp's resident dispatcher. During World War II, in addition to keeping trac of trains, the U.S. government also had him spotting for enemy airplanes.
Both pages, Stan Kistler photos

With the Hostler at Railroad Camp

It could have been just another high school summer vacation back in 1961, except that for the first time I had my own car, plus a good job. Just before classes started up again, my folks allowed me to drive off alone for a week - something I'd never done - to visit a few surviving West Coast steam operations and take photographs. My main destination was Railroad Camp, but I stopped along the way to see other lines, such as the idle West Side Lumber Company, a couple of operating Pickering Shays, the Sierra Railway's nostalgic setting at Jamestown, a lone Shay up the Feather River, even a "Prairie" tanker from the woods switching Portland's stockyards. That was a favorite hangout for my friend Jack Holst, who got us into the engine's cab for an industrial trackage ride. He was the one responsible for encouraging this trip up the coast providing me with written suggestions and directions.

There was also a letter on my dresser since sent the previous spring from the Rayonier offices, plus an article by Stan Kistler called "Loggers and Lokeys" in April 1960 *Trains* Magazine. The days of steam at Railroad Camp were numbered; a few months after my visit, Rayonier held a symbolic "End of an Era" ceremony, in which two steam engines brought their log trains part way down the mainline from Crane Creek, then turned them over to two freshly painted green and yellow Baldwin diesels bought from the Southern Pacific R.R. But in the summer of 1961 Railroad Camp still had an all steam roster.....

So, my schedule brought me to Hoquiam on a Sunday afternoon, with plans to spend part of the following day at Railroad Camp. Jack said that with lack of time it would be best just to watch the action there, instead of trying to follow trains through the dense woods, seldom catching sight of them from the highway. Since it was a weekend, the town office was closed, so I couldn't sign any waivers, but the lure of Railroad Camp was too much to ignore once I got that close, so I drove north from Hoquiam on U.S. Highway 101, winding through thick green forests of western Washington's Olympic peninsula, I was reassured of being on the right road by a sign that read;

THIS IS THE GRAYS HARBOR TREE FARM
A RAYONIER OPERATION
PREVENT FIRES

At a gravel road a few miles further I saw a yellow and white sign saying:

RAYONIER INCORPORATED
RAILROAD CAMP

An arrow pointed the way; soon I pulled my '56 Dodge to a stop in the midst of a brightly painted community of red wooden buildings, old railroad cars and - in the background - several shiny black steam engines. Green trees and bushes grew all around this place, giving it a rustic appearance seldom seen at rail terminals of this size. There were six steam engines parked on various tracks, which was a lot at one place in 1961.

Before I could figure out what to do next, I heard the chuffing sounds of a steam locomotive moving softly along. For a moment or two I thought I was daydreaming, but the sound came closer, somewhere through the trees to my right. There it was, Tank Mallet No. 110, rolling backwards on what turned out to be the mainline track, coming to a stop at a switch just a few feet from where I stood.

A young hatless fellow in denim overalls and jacket climbed down from the cab and walked over to line the switch. He smiled when he saw me; I told him hello; then he went back up into the cab and mesmerized me as he opened the engine's cylinder cocks and eased it forward ever so gently, two sets of three drive wheels each flashing uniformly in the bight sunlight. In that fashion he inched his charge about 50 feet to a little shack with a black, oily pipe, where he stopped, got up on the tender and added some fuel. He was apparently on the engine all alone, which seemed strange considering what a big size it was.

This turned out to be the Railroad Camp hostler - one of those people you may meet only once for a short while, but they manage to leave you with a lifelong impression. Our time together was so brief that I don't even recall his name. We shook hands in the cab of Mallet No. 14 and I was quite awed by the situation. He'd called me over when he got finished with No. 110 and asked if I wanted to go for a ride on an engine. He said it

RAYONIER
INCORPORATED

Eighth and Levee, Hoquiam, Washington

Mail Address - Box 539

March 22, 1961

At the end of August this year we will be operating half a dozen steam locomotives and you will be most welcome to visit the operation to see and photograph them. We operate on a five day week, Monday through Friday, and request that when you make your visit you call at our office at 8th & Levee Streets in Hoquiam before proceeding out to our Railroad Camp. We will require you to sign a waiver of liability form, a copy of which you will take with you for identification.

In case you have not had one, we are enclosing a copy of our booklet, "End of an Era".

Yours very truly,

RAYONIER INCORPORATED
Northwest Timber Division

J K Lewis

(Left, above and below) Railroad Camp on a quiet summer day in 1961, with Mallet No. 120 and Tank Mallet No. 110 waiting for the hostler to come service them for the next morning's work.
(Right) The tender of Mikado No. 70 has just been filled with water, the last of it still splashing from the end of the metal spout as it gets raised up out of the way, creaking and groaning in the process.
(Opposite) King of the Road! My friend the hostler sits proudly on the engineer's seat of Rayonier's powerful 2-6-6-2 No. 14, whose shiny black boiler is aimed down the open mainline, with no one to challenge his going for the next 30-some miles. But alas, it's Sunday afternoon and the engine will only be moved a short distance to one of the shop tracks, where an older fellow and his crew will come in the morning to take her for a real mainline run. Meanwhile, two of us shared some pleasant and memorable trackside camaraderie in the roomy cab of that steaming beast; a short taste of life in the heart of Railroad Camp.
Both pages, AHW photos

vas No. 14's turn for a drink of water at the tank and for fuel oil. I'd been in the cabs of a ew other live steam engines, but none were near as spacious as this one, nor did they ave such immense boilers looming up ahead. The hostler said I should sit in the fireman's seat, then we went to the tank for water, before backing to the oil spout. He told ne he still had No. 120 and No. 70 to service, calling the engines "lokeys," as did many ther logging railroaders in those days.

With the variety of lenses and fast films now available, it's hard not to wish for a rerun of those couple hours with the Railroad Camp hostler, this time to record every move. Oh, I took a few shots with my fixed-lens 35 mm cameras alright, both black and white and colour. But perhaps more important, the experience helped make Railroad Camp one of the most memorable places of its kind in my heart. It was like visiting with a friend and seeing him run a few engines on his model railroad layout. There was none of the pressure of normal everyday railroading, nor anyone else around to enforce the usual rules against outsiders riding on trains. It was dark by the time we finished and I drove back out to the highway, then to my hotel room in Hoquiam, having gotten much more out of that afternoon than ever expected.

(Above and above right) The bell is ringing on No. 14, as the mighty Mallet slowly works her way through Railroad Camp with a load of logs from the reload at Crane Creek, while No. 2 sits idle on the adjacent shop track. It's August 1961, the final summer before diesels.

Steam in a Foggy Forest

On Monday morning in that summer of 1961, Railroad Camp was shrouded in deep, dark clouds that kept pouring down heavy showers of rain. In addition, it was still fire season, so the logging trains went out on the line early, leaving Railroad Camp well before daylight. A great opportunity for the user of multiple flash perhaps, but that was beyond a school boy's league. Instead, I settled for some grainy fast-film shots in between the showers, plus a few choice scenes in colour. Fortunately, the rain caused things like rails, ties and engines to shine, which somewhat helped the difficulty. For me, this photo session was further complicated by the disappearance of all the black and white negatives sometime after a little booklet I wrote about Rayonier had been published, with only the few prints on these pages being left with me now.

(Above) Sometime after No. 14 has gone, a whistle at the south end announces the arrival of sister Mallet No. 120, coming back to Railroad Camp from the log dump at New London with a string of empty cars. The two Mallet-powered trains met somewhere out on the main line.
(Right) Rayonier's third Mallet, famous ex-Sierra No. 38, was inside the shop building for some serious work, including new staybolts being put in on that day. On my way to Railroad Camp I had seen an operating brass miniature of this engine during a visit with model railroad guru John Allen at his HO Gorre & Daphetid RR. I had also stopped by No. 38's former home on the Sierra Railroad, where the engineer of her diesel replacement painted such a dramatic picture that I sure was sorry the engine wasn't running when I finally got to see her. She eventually became Rayonier's last steam engine, sitting inoperable for many years in the yard at Crane Creek before being dismantled and shipped to new owners back down in California.
(Below) Although diesel locomotive salesmen had been at Railroad Camp several times over the years, as of 1961 little 4-wheeled No. 23 was still the only non-steam power on hand, hardly posing much threat to the reigning Mikados and Mallets.
Both pages, AHW photos

No. 70 as Camp Switcher

(Above) The weather began to clear later during that singular Monday, though by then the mainline trains were done and I had to think about heading homewards. Then No. 70 came to life over by the shops, running up to the tank for a drink of water and performing a bit of switching.

(Left) One of the shopmen has just taken a load of refuse to the dump, while No. 70 steams backwards down the caboose track to make an exchange.

(Opposite, top) One of No. 70's chores is to move around the engines being worked on in the shops. Here she's got No. 111 of the Tank Mallet duo, this one outfitted with an extra tender while No. 110 still ran alone as designed.

(Opposite, bottom) Half of the Rayonier caboose roster based at Railroad Camp is seen here, on the end of a log train in the yard at the south end. Sometimes referred to as "outhouses on wheels," they nevertheless served to keep train crews out of the rain during the 30 and 40 mile trips. They were painted boxcar red with white trim.

(Far right) An almost timeless scene at Railroad Camp, as Mikado No. 70 takes a drink at the big water tower, which for years dominated one end of this picturesque place, providing an ideal photographer's platform. This was still considered a special engine because of its many years assigned to old engineer Peggy Rogers, who treated it as if it were his own. By 1961 her boiler was no longer being blued; Peggy had retired and died, though his son Bobby still worked on her regularly. But even with her boiler painted black instead, white trim on the domes and red on the windows continued to give her a regal bearing. When Rayonier's steam era ended, No. 70 went to the Puget Sound Railroad Historical Society at Snoqualmie, Washington.

Both pages, AHW photos

Structures from another Time

bove) Over the years some of the structures at Railroad Camp changed to suit the needs f operations, but the basic layout remained about the same right till the end. Here in 1961 e mainline is in the foreground and the main shops are at the back, with one each of the ree remaining kinds of steam engines gathered around. At left is the locomotive shop, at ght is the boiler and welding shop, and in the foreground is the rigging shed for cables.

ight) Mallet No. 120 is the backdrop for this sturdy homemade crane near the boiler and achine shops.

pposite, top and below) A one-track, open-air engine shed stands empty, while nearby are arked a very ancient wooden boxcar (much altered since its Northern Pacific days) along ith one of the line's many portable camp cars, parked on the spur by the big warehouse.

ar left) A sturdy base of huge logs holds up the Railroad Camp water tank, which is of a ze more typical of larger lines than most loggers out in the woods. Although the gauge says early full at the moment, two or three of those Mallets could drain quite a bit of that in a ort time. In the early years a square water tank served lokeys down at the other end of ailroad Camp.
oth pages, AHW photos

One Last Look at Railroad Camp

(Above) It was the summer of 1967; the steam era had about come to an end, even on remote lines in the woods. Yet th atmosphere of the old days hung heavy wherever such tracks still existed. Shiny diesel No. 45 may seem a bit out of plac inside this classic vintage structure that once served as Railroad Camp's boiler repair shop for steam engines, yet shows how the tools of different eras have served mankind in places like this.

(Above left) A farewell glance into Railroad Camp's immense carpentry shop, where many wooden cars were built ove the years and overhauled, including custom made camp cars.

(Left) Nature quickly reclaims its own! Only a few years had passed since Rayonier stopped stocking lineside logger camps with supplies from this big warehouse, yet already trees and bushes were taking back over. Bypassed with a ne mainline, Railroad Camp was closed in 1968, less than a year after these photos, then torn down, after which the fore took almost everything back over.

AHW photos

(*Footnote: In 1974 a portion of the old Railroad Camp property, including the superintendent's house, was bought b Rayonier's timber division manager George V. Lonngren, who then built a modern retirement home there

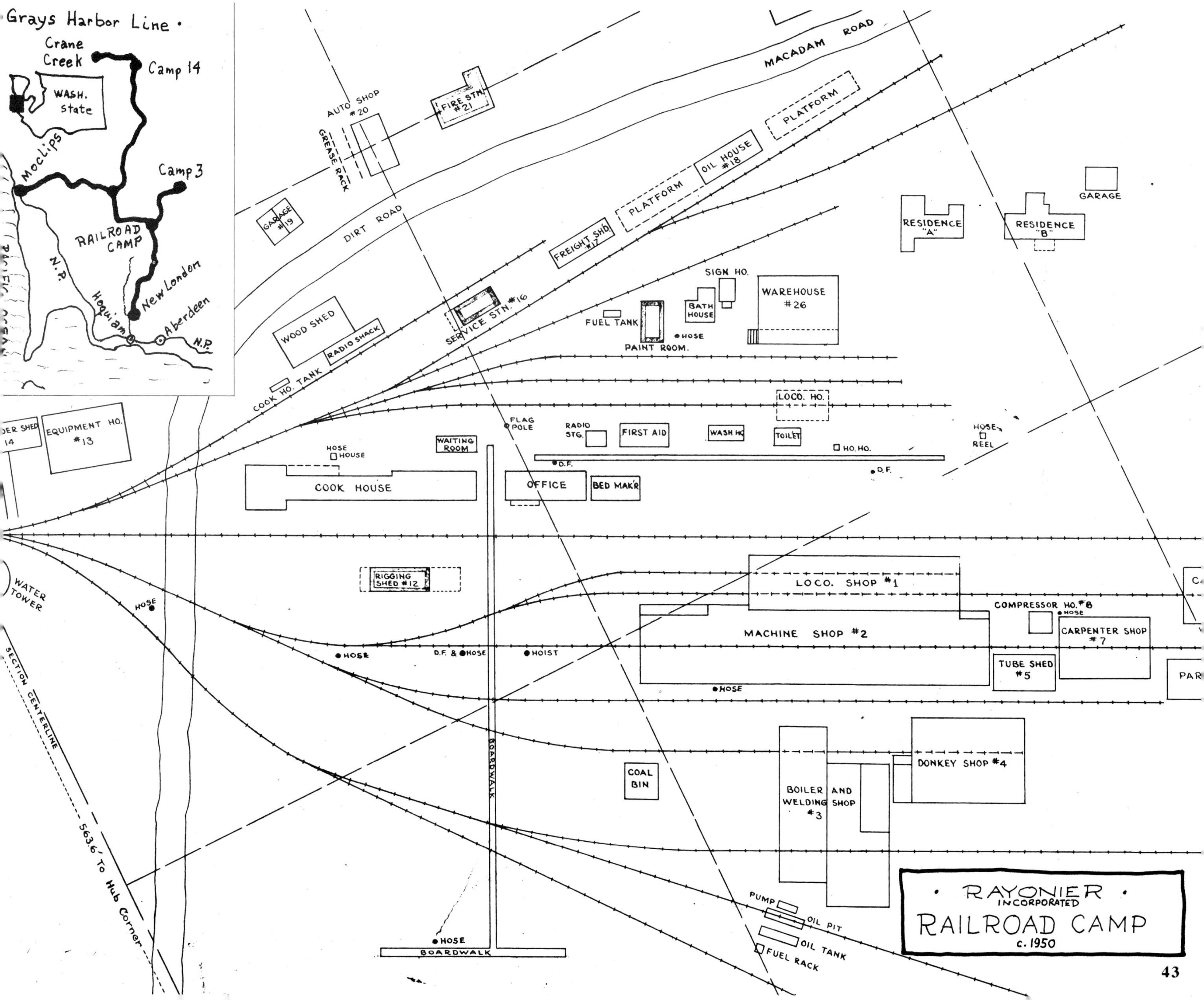

Grays Harbor Line
Crane Creek
Camp 14
WASH. State
Moclips
Camp 3
RAILROAD CAMP
N.P.
New London
Hoquiam
Aberdeen
N.P.
MACADAM ROAD
DIRT ROAD
AUTO SHOP #20
GREASE RACK
FIRE STN. #21
PLATFORM
OIL HOUSE #18
PLATFORM
FREIGHT SHD. #17
GARAGE #19
SERVICE STN. #16
WOOD SHED
RADIO SHACK
COOK HO. TANK
SIGN HO.
BATH HOUSE
FUEL TANK
HOSE
PAINT ROOM.
WAREHOUSE #26
RESIDENCE "A"
RESIDENCE "B"
GARAGE
LOCO. HO.
EQUIPMENT HO. #13
HOSE HOUSE
WAITING ROOM
FLAG POLE
RADIO STG.
FIRST AID
WASH HO
TOILET
HO. HO.
HOSE REEL
D.F.
COOK HOUSE
OFFICE
BED MAK'R
WATER TOWER
RIGGING SHED #12
LOCO. SHOP #1
COMPRESSOR HO. #8
HOSE
MACHINE SHOP #2
CARPENTER SHOP #7
HOSE
HOSE
D.F. & HOSE
HOIST
TUBE SHED #5
HOSE
SECTION CENTERLINE
5636' To Hub Corner
BOARDWALK
COAL BIN
BOILER AND WELDING SHOP #3
DONKEY SHOP #4
PUMP
OIL PIT
OIL TANK
FUEL RACK
HOSE
BOARDWALK
RAYONIER INCORPORATED
RAILROAD CAMP
c. 1950

RAILROAD CAMP'S LOKEYS:

Mikado No. 2

(Opposite, top) The Baldwin photographer took this first portrait of No. 2 when new back in 191 posed on the turntable outside the company's Philadelphia shops. She was headed for Michigan to ha logs for the Saginaw Timber Company.
H.L. Broadbelt collection

(Left) Years later, No. 2 steams in the morning rain at Railroad Camp, one of several Mikados re dent here under both Polson and Rayonier management.
Ernie Plant collection

(Opposite, below) Seventy tons is fairly light for a Mikado, so No. 2 was only good for about 20 loa on the Rayonier mainline. Once the Mallets came, she spent most of her time doing switching an other light work, or sitting by the shop as a standby. On this occasion in August 1953 she had hold o caboose at one end and an old flat car with firewood at the other, while two of her crewmen lo back towards the office at the fellows milling around the crew car. Note that at this time the o square water tank was still standing, beyond the locomotive shop.
Railway Negative Exchange/AHW collection

(Below) Headed back to Michigan! In 1962 Rayonier bought a pair of husky Baldwin diesels, which a lowed the company to retire most of the steam engines, including No. 2. A price list was offered potential purchasers, listing No. 2 at $1,540.00 (imagine what the price would be today!). A gro from Michigan immediately saw the chance to bring back home one of their own. They were to that the lokey last had an overhaul in March 1951, getting new tubes and stay bolts and that she w "only used periodically" since then. "The shop superintendent says the boiler is in good shape and the are some spare parts available." This scene shows the engine in April 1963 on the Northern Paci mainline near Missoula, Montana. Aboard her is Rayonier employee Jim Gertz, "babysitter" for t 3,000 mile journey, himself the owner of one of the company's former Willamette Shays. Speed lim for the engine was 25 mph, which meant being passed from one local freight to the next, with Ger always on the lookout for chances to buy grub or do the laundry. In the small space of her cab he ha rigged up a bed, cooking facilities and a radio. The engine became Grand Travers Northern No. then Cadillac & Lake City No. 2, then she worked for the Kettle Moraine RR and now she is back being Saginaw Lumber No. 2 at the highly regarded Mid-Continent Railway Museum in North Fre dom, Wisconsin.
Ernie Plant collection

SAGINAW TIMBER COMPANY
2
THE BALDWIN LOCOMOTIVE WORKS.
4230

45
P O L S O N L O G G I N G Co
HG Nelson
Photo

RAILROAD CAMP LOKEYS:

Prairie No. 45

(Right) One of the first locomotives to be bought new by the Polson Brothers was this pretty 2-6-2, turned out by Baldwin in 1906. A 44-tonner with 44 inch driving wheels, she was rated as having 16,700 pounds of tractive effort.
H.L. Broadbelt collection

(Opposite) Not long after going to work on the Polson line, No. 45 is seen with her crew out in the Washington woods. The drivers still show some of their pin-striping, but the tender is beginning to show the daily wear and tear of a woodburner. Whoever designed that stack left his mark on railroad history for bad taste; compare it to the one they put on new at the factory. It must not have worked too good either, since it doesn't show in any other scenes. However, the "coffee can" style of spark arrester most common on this line in later years could have originated from the top half of this stack.
H.G. Nelson photo/Rayonier collection

(Bottom right) By 1952 No. 45 was down to standby duties at Railroad Camp, now and then still doing a bit of switching or trackwork. The arrival of more Mallets not long after this put her out of business, but fortunately the company took her into Hoquiam and put her on display, a symbol of more than 50 years' operation on the Polson and Rayonier lines.
Railway Negative Exchange/AHW collection

RAILROAD CAMP LOKEYS:

Mikado No. 90

(Above) Heaviest Mikado operating out of Railroad Camp was 86-ton No. 90, seen here new at the Baldwin shops in 1926. She was rated at 35,700 lbs. of tractive effort, more than twice that of No. 45.
(Below) Another rainy-day engine portrait taken in front of Railroad Camp's main locomotive shop, this one showing No. 90 steamed and ready for work.
(Below right) Still shiny and well-cared for, here's No. 90 making her official last run on March 12, 1962 as part of Rayonier's "End of an Era" ceremony. She is seen at Humptulips with a load of logs from Crane Creek. When put up for sale a few weeks later, the Oregon Memorial Steam Train Association offered to pay $1,980.00, but in a friendly gesture Rayonier let them have this engine for a token $10.
John Poulsen collection

RAILROAD CAMP LOKEYS:
Consolidation No. 99

Above) Baldwin built 2-8-0 No. 99 in 1905 for the Polson Brothers, where she spent her whole ife. Here she is seen at the south end of Railroad Camp in August 1953, bringing a caboose down o the trains in the yard. The water tank is at the left.

Below) A few months earlier in the same year, No. 99 is seen at the standard portrait location y the shop. Although still well-kept, the lokey was in its final season of work as a switcher and tand-by, soon to be displaced by the mainline Mikados after the purchase of the Mallets. The ow status of No. 99 by this time was evident by the unusual lack of company name on the tender. 'olson's name was covered over, but Rayonier had already been in charge for five years. The ngine was eventually scrapped at Railroad Camp.
3oth, Railway Negative Exchange/AHW collection

RAILROAD CAMP LOKEYS:

Mikado No. 101

(Above) Locomotive histories are often filled with interesting twists and turns. For instance, two consecutive 2-8-2's turned out by Baldwin in 1912 included Polson Logging No. 101, seen here upon completion, and Saginaw Lumber No. 2, which was later bought by Polson and left its Michigan home after a few years to rejoin No. 101 as a working partner at Railroad Camp.
H.L. Broadbelt collection

(Below) At the locomotive shop in 1956, No. 101 is steamed and ready during her final seasons of work. By the time of my 1961 visit she was at the end of the riptrack, on the edge of Railroad Camp, being slowly dismantled, then finally scrapped.
Railway Negative Exchange/
AHW collection

RAILROAD CAMP
LOKEYS:

Shay 191 & Mallet 3100

(Above) In the late 1920's the Polson Brothers bought two big three-truck Shays to replace lighter geared power used mainly on rough and steep branches and spurs out in the woods. At 94 tons, No. 191 was the heaviest of these, purchased new from Lima Locomotive Works in 1929. By the time of this 1952 photo at Railroad Camp, logging spurs were a thing of the past, so Shay Nos. 91 and 191 were mainly assigned to bring logs down from Camp 3 to the mainline. This engine was scrapped a few years later, while sister No. 91 was sold to the Feather River Railway in California for parts. By the way, it would be interesting to learn what system the Polson Brothers used for numbering their new lokeys (second-hand engines generally kept the numbers they arrived with).

(Right) After some 30 years of mainline service for the Northern Pacific Railroad, this brute was brought to Railroad Camp to usher in a new motive power era on the Polson logging line, the use of articulated locomotives. Baldwin built No. 3100 in 1910, with a weight of more than 150 tons. She was the heaviest engine ever used out of Railroad Camp, but being a saturated type, her tractive effort of 58,000 pounds was later outdone by the newer and lighter Mallets, all of which were superheated. According to Railroad Camp legend, Polson paid $10,000 for No. 3100 (she kept her NP number), then turned down a much greater offer when World War II traffic caused NP officials to try buying her back. This 1951 picture shows her next to No. 90 at Railroad Camp, where she was scrapped in 1959.

Both, Railway Negative Exchange/AHW collection

(Above left) Here's No. 110 at Railroad Camp in 1964, by which time a tender had been added to make longer runs. At 111 tons, this engine was rated at 37,500 lbs. of tractive effort. For size comparison we have Mallet No. 38 on the next track, weighing some 146 tons and pulling 59,600 lbs. No. 110 was sold in 1969 to a National Railroad Historical Society chapter in Promontory, Utah.
John Cummings photo/John Elwood collection

(Below) The Weyerhaeuser Timber Company used a number of large locomotives, including a pair of saddletank Mallet compounds that were both No. 110. Here is the first of the two, built by Baldwin in 1927 with serial number 60561. The second No. 110 came 10 years later and must have provided some confusing times to company accountants along with the crews.

(Above right) This was Weyerhaeuser's "second" No. 110, built by Baldwin in 1937 with serial number 62064, weighing in at some 120 tons and rated at 42,500 lbs. tractive effort. At Rayonier she became No. 111, first of the pair to receive a spare tender; she is seen here at Railroad Camp in May 1960. In 1969 she was sold to the California Western Railroad, where her saddle tanks were removed and she was put into tourist passenger service. In a further twist of fate, California Western then made her No. 45, which had been the number of a Railroad Camp running mate.
John Poulsen collection

Mallet No. 120

(Top) Also bought by Rayonier from Weyerhaeuser in 1954 was Mallet No. 120, seen here brand new in 1936 outside the Baldwin shops.
H.L. Broadbelt collection

(Bottom) About five years after coming to Rayonier, No. 120 is seen out on the line with a caboose and 59 empty log cars, approaching one of the few highway crossings between Railroad Camp and Crane Creek. On June 14, 1962 Rayonier offered this engine for sale at $2,640.00 saying it had not been operated for a while. A few weeks later the price dropped to $2,500, but this was for the engine without tender, which had meanwhile been assigned to serve as a fire car on trains hauled by diesels. She was eventually sold to a scrap dealer in nearby Aberdeen and cut up.
David Wilkie photo

RAILROAD CAMP LOKEYS:

Mallet No. 14

(Above) Bloedel Donovan Lumber Mills was another large company that used a variety of locomotives on its logging railroads. Mallet No. 14 was built in 1927 and 10 years later went to work on a new line built by the company in Washington's Clallam County. Starting at the port town of Sekiu, on the Strait of Juan de Fuca, this line eventually went about 40 miles into the woods near Forks. The purchase of this operation by Rayonier in 1945 included several lokeys, including No. 14. When the line was dieselized in 1956, No. 14 was put aboard a barge at Sekiu, towed down the Pacific Coast to Grays Harbor, then up the Hoquiam River to New London, where it was lifted back on tracks and sent to Railroad Camp.
H.L. Broadbelt collection

(Left) Highballing down the mainline towards Railroad Camp is No. 14 in 1959, when she and her two sisters still did most of the log hauling work. In 1962 she was offered for sale by Rayonier for $2,860.00, with a note saying that she was in good operating condition and could be had with "spare tires and a considerable stock of parts." Sadly, this was in a time before the historic value of such a machine was widely appreciated; when no buyers came forward, she was sent to Aberdeen with No. 120 and scrapped.
Ernie Plant collection

RAILROAD CAMP LOKEYS:

Sierra No. 38

(Above) The only survivor of Rayonier's four big Mallets (not counting the saddletankers) is No. 38, which has also been the most famous of them. Built in 1934 as Weyerhaeuser No. 4, a distant sister to No. 120, she later went to California's popular Mother Lode shortline, which is when she began to be called Sierra 38. In 1955 she pulled a special farewell train on that railroad, turning the consist over to diesels, a dubious honour she had again in 1962 during Rayonier's "End of an Era" ceremony. Perhaps it was her Sierra fame that made her stand out at Rayonier as well, so that she was for many years the last steam engine on the property. She is now privately owned in California.

(Right) Everyone who has heard Stan Kistler's album "Whistles in the Woods" knows that Rayonier engineers were noted for making beautiful railroad music with those melodious five-chime whistles, sometimes carrying out the sounds for half a minute or more, after which the echoes continued through the woods even longer. Although the engine number on this train at Humptulips was not recorded, we can be sure it was a Mallet by the long string of cars.

Both, Ernie Plant collection

Out on the Line With

No. 120

bove) It was hard to beat this scenic site for photographing Rayonier trains on the Gray's Harbor line. Mallet No. 120 is crossing Prairie Creek trestle at Mile 42 with a string of empties for Crane Creek Read on April 27, 1959. Because much of the railroad went through thick woods some distance from any road or highway it was difficult to get action shots. It was best to pick out a spot like this well in advance
d then wait for the train, straining over the sounds of rushing water to hear the distant warning whistle, long, low and melodic.

pposite, lower left) Here's No. 120 at the same place on the next day, heading for Railroad Camp with 54 loads of logs. Note the silhouette of engineer Clark Pennick up in that big cab. Also, overnight rains
ve swollen Prairie Creek quite a bit from the scene above.

pposite, upper left) On another trip during that same time period, No. 120 has 34 loads as she rolls south across the Humptulips River on a new steel bridge. Built in 1955 to replace an old wooden structure,
is bridge was from 50 to 60 feet high and about a quarter mile long. A public picnic area under its south end was fortunate never to suffer any accidents, in spite of all the log traffic going by overhead.

ar left) At Crane Creek reload on May 13, 1958, No. 120 pushes a string of empties up ahead for log loading. For many years a switcher based here had full time work, but towards the end each road engine
d its own switching.

l four, David Wilkie photos

111
111

Camp 14

Living History in the Woods

(Right) Rayonier's Camp 14 was one of the last places in North America where crews of loggers lived aboard camp cars in a moveable village built to roll on tracks. Here's most of the camp in 1956 as seen from the tender of Sierra Mallet No. 38, having just arrived with a trainload of logs from Crane Creek, seven miles back. In the past there were spurs running out into the woods from here, so train crews lived in these cars as well; one or two engines were usually kept on hand. Dirt roads and log trucks eventually became cheaper for this work, so the logs were trucked to Crane Creek for reloading onto trains.

Meeting of the Mallets.

(Opposite) Looking ahead of No. 38 on the same train, southbound on the mainline, with saddletank No. 111 parked on the siding.

Both, Stan Kistler photos

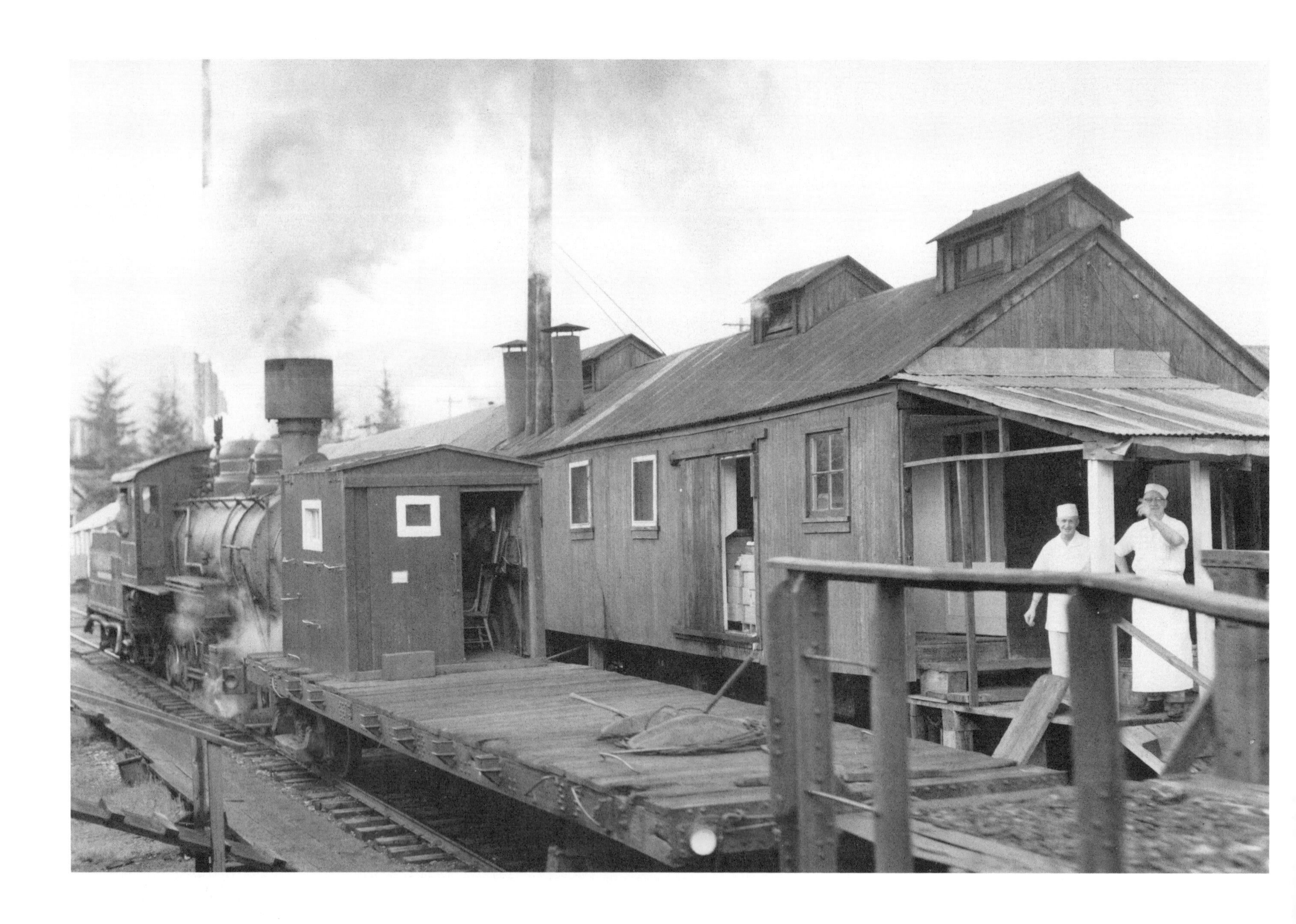

The Camp 14 Cookhouse

)pposite) The cooks at Camp 14 stand outside their kitchen-on-wheels to give Mi-ıdo No. 70 and its train a rollby inspection in 1956. At this time Rayonier still oper-ed its 15 mile Moclips branch, which connected with a Northern Pacific branch-ıe at the coast. No. 70 is seen leaving Humptulips for Moclips to bring a load of dar to the NP interchange. When this branch was closed a few months later, the ıyonier line became isolated and any equipment going in or out had to be floated ı a barge, including locomotives and their fuel.

ight) The same two cooks are seen busy at work inside their kitchen car, a logging ilroad's version of a dining car on wheels. Some 60 to 70 men still lived at Camp and the meals served were equal to logging cookhouse legends. Big steaks, home-ade bread, fresh vegetables and lots of strong black coffee were mainstays, along th dozens of freshly made pies, all of which cost the men 85 cents a piece. After a ırd day's work you can imagine their response when the sound of the cooks' trian-e bell was heard ringing through the camp.

bove) Agent and timekeeper at Camp 14 for many years was Dick Lewis, seen re having a visit on the steps of the camp office while his dog Brownie occupies e mainline. Among other duties, the dog was supposed to keep woods bears away om the camp kitchen and garbage, but in those days it was often considered easier st to shoot most wild animals that hung around.
th pages, Stan Kistler photos

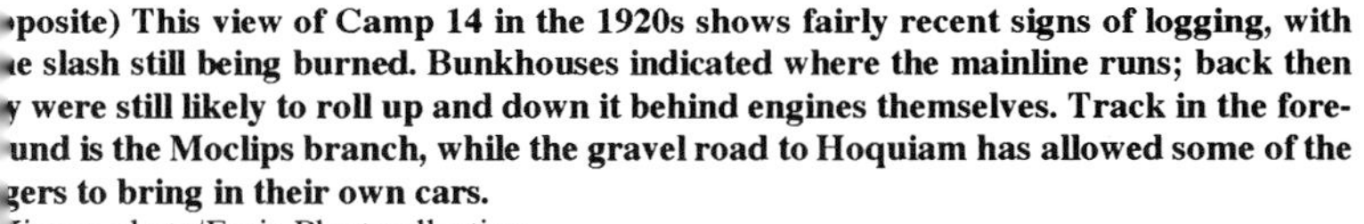

posite) This view of Camp 14 in the 1920s shows fairly recent signs of logging, with e slash still being burned. Bunkhouses indicated where the mainline runs; back then y were still likely to roll up and down it behind engines themselves. Track in the fore- und is the Moclips branch, while the gravel road to Hoquiam has allowed some of the gers to bring in their own cars.
Kinsey photo/Ernie Plant collection

is page) Three views of camp cars and other buildings at Camp 14 in 1963, during the seasons of its regular use. Note in the upper right view how the spur track on the it has been covered with boards for regular foot traffic. It had been years since any hese buildings were last moved and most of them were scrapped where they stood. yonier camp cars do survive in a few places, however, including several at the Camp Logging Exhibit in nearby Tacoma, which also operates a Shay and other things.
three, AHW photos

90

ITT-Rayonier in the Diesel Era

(Opposite) Crews exchange friendly greetings as logging trains meet on Rayonier's modernized mainline between Crane Creek Reload and the New London log dump on June 25, 1980. The southbound train of logs is being led by yellow and green No. 90, former Southern Pacific No. 5275, a 1200-hp unit built by Baldwin in 1952 and renumbered to honor former Rayonier Mikado No. 90. Photo was taken from the caboose of an empty northbound train being hauled by Baldwin No. 76, which honoured the U.S. Bicentennial and carried the name "Spirit of 76," plus a red, white and blue paint job. By this time the former Polson Brothers logging line belonged to the International Telephone and Telegraph company and was operated under the name ITT-Rayonier.
(Left) Engineer Bobby Rogers looks from the fireman's side of his engine as the rear brakeman waves from the caboose of the other train.
(Below) So long, brakeman! The date of this trip is etched in our family's minds because it was the seventh birthday of son Okan and he was given a special treat. Engine cab rides have been available on some railroads to responsible adults, but seldom to young kids. However, while I was signing my waiver forms for the ride, Rayonier's George Lonngren learned that it was Okan's birthday, so he said I couldn't leave him standing behind on such a special occasion, which indeed it turned out to be.
Both pages, AHW photos

ITT RAYONIER

(Opposite) The world may have changed a lot between 1903 and 1980, but all through that time logs from forests were brought here to New London by trains, then dumped into the Hoquiam River and floated downstream a few miles for sawmill processing. On this foggy morning, ITT Rayonier's Bicentennial lokey No. 76 has just dropped off another load and is about to head north with a string of empties, plus the watercar in the foreground which was always in the train in case of fire. The track-mounted log unloaders of the past were long gone, replaced by a monstrous overhead unloading crane (seen in the far distance) that was supported by steel girders above the tracks and part of the river. Instead of the old system of simply knocking the logs into the river, this unit picked up a whole carload (one every two minutes) and lowered it gently into the water, allowing the formation of uniform log rafts and the quicker separation of logs for pulp and nonpulp use. The unit was also used to load and unload barges bringing supplies to the landlocked railroad, including the star-spangled diesel and its three mates. A similar crane was used at Crane Creek for loading up the logs.

(Below) A roster of some 600 log cars was in use on Rayoniers's Grays Harbor line during the final decades, representing a variety of origins and lengths, including this fairly short example seen at Crane Creek in 1980.

(Right) Recalling the regular water stops made in steam days, this diesel-powered train has paused to fill its water car at a site not far from the recently-closed Railroad Camp. This view was taken from the caboose platform, right behind the engine.

Both pages, AHW photos

Stars on the Birthday Train

(Left) There's the birthday boy himself, seven-year old Okan, waving from the fireman's seat, where he rode most of the trip. Of course, the stars were for a much bigger birthday - the United States Bicentennial in 1976 - as was the engine number "76." We're stopped here for clearance by radio before entering Crane Creek which allowed time for a quick picture from the ground.
(Above) Bobby Rogers, born and raised on this "railroad through the woods," doing what to him came almost naturally, the running of an engine.
(Below) Part of the birthday trip was spent back in the caboose, with the conductor and brakeman, who used the time to visit and eat, while still keeping an eye on the train. Their main work was at the two terminals, switching the loads and empties.
All, AHW photos

A Tribute to the Final Logging Trains

(Above) For those of us who regularly share the highways with logging trucks, this scene shows such a contrast that we must wonder if the change was really progress. A southbound train of logs is seen on the day after Okan's birthday, rolling along at 35 mph behind ITT Rayonier's diesel No. 90, the Baldwin's bright green and yellow flanks reflecting from a trackside pool while the surrounding damp woods seem to deepen the throbbing chant of its motors. And thus the logs went off to market, while the highways were safer drive.
A&OHW photo

(Above) Even a wide-angle lens hasn't captured all the loaded log cars parked here in the reload yard at Crane Creek in June 1980. This was one of the last places where railroad logging was carried on at such a scale. We're looking from the cab through the doorway of No. 76, with its distinctive Baldwin brow at the left. A hazy sun is setting on the scene; there will not be too many more afternoons here like this.

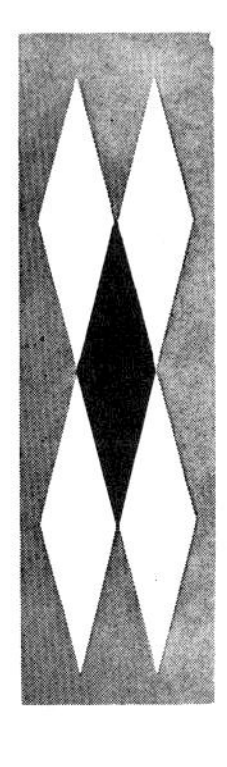

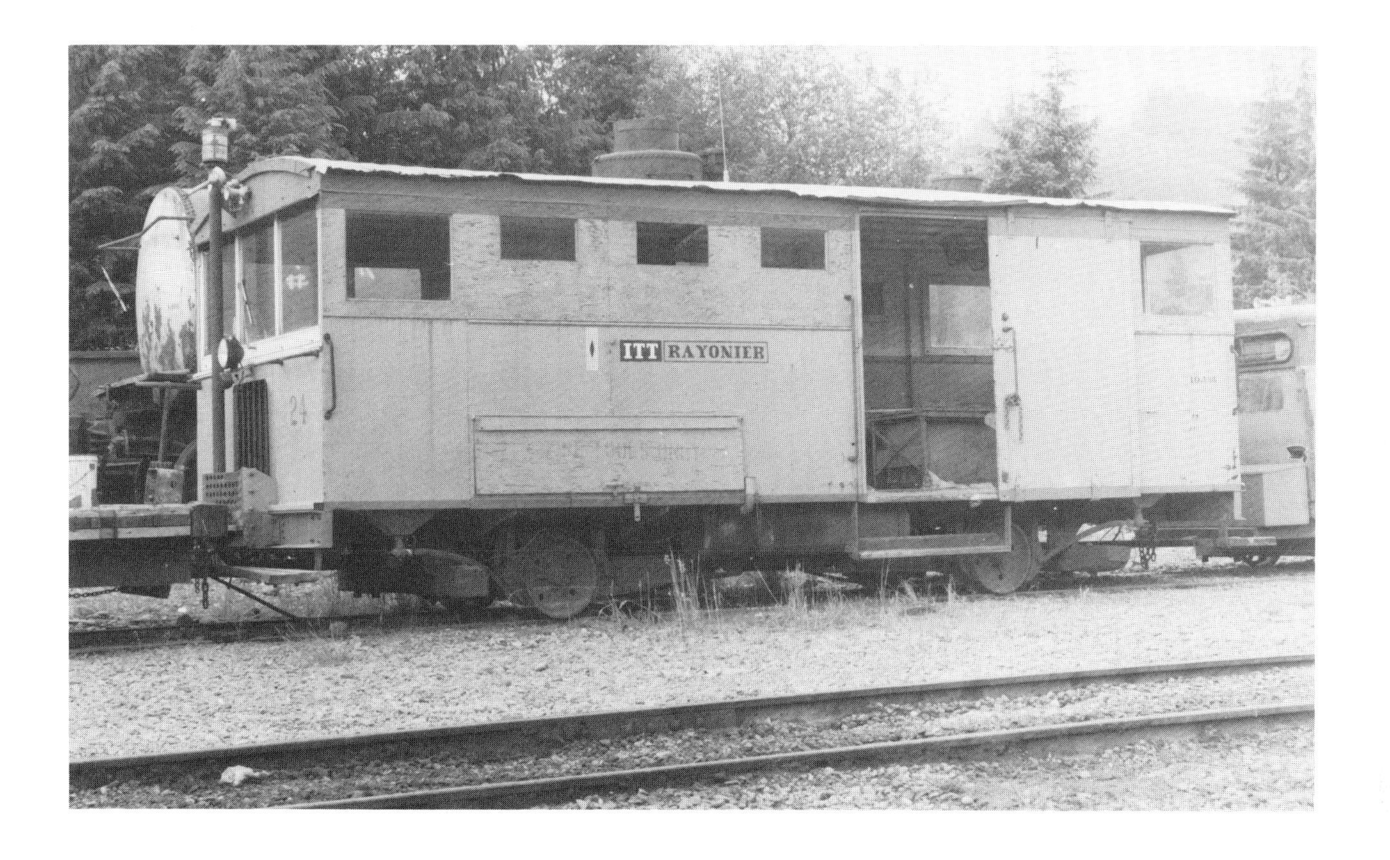

(Above) Among the unique pieces of rolling stock in use on this railroad right to the end was Crew Car No. 24, which had many predecessors down through the years. Powered with a truck motor, this substantial unit was often used to haul fire crews to points along the line.

(Below) Car No. 21 is about the right size for a seven-year old, who now has a rig something like this by his home. The archbar-trucked water car in back was a main-line tanker running all over North America for a good part of the early 1900s before coming out to the woods.
Both pages, AHW photos

45

They Were Still Built by Baldwin

)pposite) Arriving and departing crews have a short at at Crane Creek, while Bobby Rogers looks down om his window aboard No. 76. Nos. 45 and 90 are e other two engines.

bove right) Here is the replacement for Railroad amp - a single, huge, characterless shop building hose interior served the four Baldwin diesel engines ong with numerous logging trucks, cats and other achinery. The elaborate contraption on the right re- aced the old time section crews and work trains ce pulled by the likes of Ten-Wheelers.

elow right) It takes quite a crew to load sand onto e of those mighty diesels! Let's see, one guy drove e forklift that brought the box of fresh sand; the guy th the bucket is the young fireman doing one of his ties; Okan is the little guy watching him; but that ill leaves four whose purposes are unaccounted for, us the photographer. Quite a big deal in the woods, I ess, these train arrivals. Note the lettering on the d, white and blue engine, including the smaller script 'reedom" above Okan's head. The green and yellow No. 90 was more in harmony with the forest back- ound.

oth pages, AHW photos

Final Seasons on the Grays Harbor Line

(Left) Compare this setting at Crane Creek in 1980 with some of the Railroa Camp photos from the early decades to see the evolution of this particular lo ging railroad. It's not likely anything in this scene existed back in the Polso days, not even the tracks, yet that home-painted "No. 45" on the engine a sures us it's still the same old line. Two styles of heavy-duty steel flatcars ar seen, both retired from Northern Pacific mainline service. The transfer tabl in foreground served two shop tracks and was unique for a logging railroa Little gas-powered No. 23 is still the shop switcher, as in steam days at Rai road Camp.
(Above) A much-modified tender stood as silent symbol of the steam era a Crane Creek, painted green and yellow for water service. "No. 1" in the fore ground looks like the surviving remnants of a vintage machine, still put to goo use.
(Opposite) That the workers continued to have pride in this logging railroa right to the end is evidenced by the way they took care of the equipment. A though somewhat scuffed and scraped from passing trees, the unnumbere wooden caboose coupled to No. 90 shows distinct character, handsome in i matching green and yellow livery, plus white trim and black lettering. Tw other photos show the final version of this railroad's cabooses, a wood-frame metal car (again unnumbered) with modern windows and a bit of "the wester touch" in metalwork.
Both pages, A&OHW photos

ITT RAYONIER

ITT
Rayonier

The Clallam Line
Rayonier's *Other* Logging Railroad

(Above) On the foggy coast of the Strait of Juan de Fuca, along northern Washington's Olympic Peninsula, there was a logging railroad that ended on a wharf. Its 40 miles of tracks began in 1937 - rather late in the logging railroad era - to serve holdings of the Bloedel-Donovan Lumber Mills, an operation that used a varied lot of Shays, Heislers and Climaxes. Rayonier bought this operation in 1945, with three Mallets then handling mainline duties while geared power continued to work the branches. The 1956 purchase of a new pair of Baldwin-Lima-Hamilton 1200-hp diesels brought early dieselization, though steam stayed on a while longer; some has been preserved. Log trains on this operation ended up here at this dock in Sekiu, where the trees were dumped into the water and floated from there to the mills.
John Cummings photo/John Elwood collection

(Left) Square-tank Mallet No. 8 blasts out of town with her caboose and a string of empties, while the crew waves at a fellow Rayonier employee snapping this picture. The seaside calm of Sekiu was momentarily overcome by the awesome sounds of steam engine stack talk, as this husky articulated put her 12 driving wheels to the steel. No. 8 has since become the private lokey of longtime logging engineer Pete Replinger, who keeps it in the state of Washington.
Jim Gertz photo

(Opposite, top left) Rayonier's Clallam line had its shops and main yard at Sekiu, not far from the unloading dock. Employees were on strike at the time of this 1963 view, so nothing was moving. Two diesels and two steam engines were locked up inside.
AHW photo

(Top right) Rayonier's Baldwin-built No. 202 was seen switching an old tank car in the yard at Sekiu in 1961 with shops and a truss-rod car in the background.

(Bottom right) A Shay on the shore, as No. 4 switches cars in front of company buildings and engine facilities at Sekiu in the 1950s.
Jim Gertz photo

(Bottom left) Shay No. 4 was built by Willamette in 1924 as Long-Bell Lumber No. 701. Seen here at the end of a branch known as the 12-E line, she is framed by an immense homemade rig that was hooked to a big diesel motor and used for loading the log cars.
Al Mitchell photo

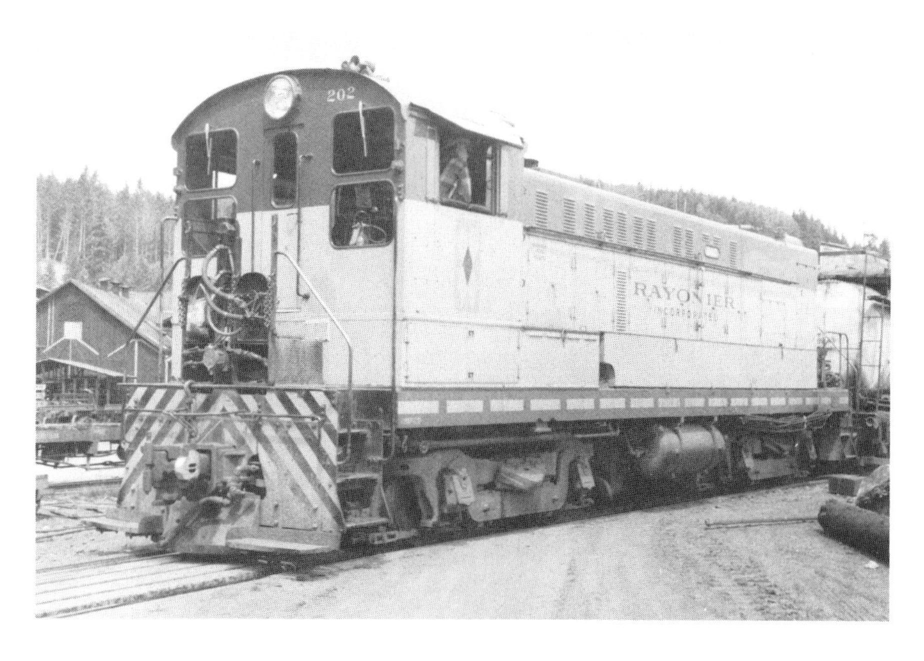
202
RAYONIER
INCORPORATED

RAYONIER

Dedicated to Jim and Pete

(Below right) Here's one that was saved - by the photographer, yet! Rayonier No. 2 was the last lokey built (in 1929) by the Willamette Iron & Steel Works of Portlland, Ore. and thus a genuine Northwest native. One of her final runs on the Clallam line was with this work train. Jim Gertz photo

(Above) Wooden caboose No. 4 crosses a wooden trestle on the Clallam line. Jim Gertz photo

(Above right) A homemade yard switcher at Sekiu in 1963. AHW photo

(Opposite, top left)Turnstile jib on the dock at Sekiu was used to knock logs from cars down into the harbor. Crane on left helped load supplies from barges on to railroad cars. AHW photo

(Opposite, top right) An outbound train of empties follows Mallet No. 8 along the shore of the Pacific Ocean as it leaves Sekiu for the woods in the 1950s. Jim Gertz photo

(Opposite, bottom left) Four-wheeled cabooses don't get much more funky than this one, parked outside the Sekiu shops in 1963. AHW photo

(Opposite, bottom right) Here's another lokey that was saved, this time by Pete Replinger. Perhaps someday Jim and Pete will treat us to a thorough Rayonier history, using their two lokeys for inspiration. Jim Gertz photo

RAYONIER
INCORPORATED

(Above) What a disappointment! Having grown to know the famous Sierra Mallet No. 38 from frequent browsings through dad's books, seven-year old Okan Hungry Wolf was quite let down when I brought him to Rayonier's Crane Creek reload where he first met the engine. He'd seen other steam engines before this one, but they were well cared for, nicely painted, mostly still operable. Now, here was this proud, big beast of a 2-6-6-2, as sort of a hulk rusting in a dusty yard of diesels and modern logging trucks. While I went up to explore the tender, he sat down on the engineer's footboard, a scene of dejection. But, - not to worry - his smile returned after spending a few hours riding in the cab of one of Rayonier's big Baldwin diesels with engineer Bobby Rogers, who used to run No. 38.
AHW photo

(Opposite) Here's Sierra No. 38 in brighter times, on Rayonier Incorporated's mainline running through a stretch of Washington state's vast forests. We're at Camp 14 in the late 1950s, a time when the world still moved slow enough out here to make steam engines worth operating, and to have loggers living aboard little houses built to run on railroad tracks. This was certainly an operation with a lot of character; a piece of heritage now gone forever.
Ernie Plant collection